TIPS

Improving Acoustics
for Music Teaching

By
Harold P. Geerdes

Music Educators National Conference

Table of Contents

Foreword

The Music Educators National Conference (MENC) has created the TIPS series to provide music educators with a variety of ideas on a wide range of practical subjects. Each TIPS booklet is a compilation of methods, ideas, and suggestions that have been successful in the music classroom. MENC has designed this quick-reference series to be used as a starting point for creating and adapting projects for your particular situation.

TIPS: Improving Acoustics for Music Teaching is a concise manual designed to help music educators upgrade their existing music facilities or design new ones correctly.

Introduction

The school music program requires facilities for many different types of activities including:
- Classroom instruction
- Individual teaching and practice
- Small-ensemble rehearsal
- Large-ensemble rehearsal
- Performance

These facilities are an extension of performers' instruments or voices. A poor instrument or voice can sound quite acceptable or even good in a room with favorable acoustics. However, even Pavarotti or a Stradivarius violin will sound less than magnificent in an acoustically poor space. The importance of the room as an integral part of the sound-producing process cannot be overemphasized. Unfortunately, music, more than any other subject in the school or college curriculum, is often taught in rooms not properly designed for it.

A good music space has certain essential requirements, most of which are different from those of the ordinary academic classroom. The requirements include:
- Good listening conditions
- Accommodation of both low and high levels of sound power
- Especially quiet ventilation
- Quiet lighting systems
- Isolation of sound intrusion from adjoining spaces

The music teacher should be especially concerned about the quality of the rooms in which he or she works. Music educators must be persistent about upgrading existing facilities or being certain special care is exercised when new ones are planned. The rooms should be assets to the school music program—not liabilities.

* * *

Some Fundamentals of
Room Acoustics

To think constructively about the rooms where music is taught (classrooms), rehearsed (rehearsal and practice rooms), and performed (auditoriums, gymnasiums, multipurpose rooms), it helps to have an understanding of the basic concepts of room acoustics. "Room acoustics" is different from "music acoustics." Room acoustics is the study of how sound responds in a particular architectural environment and music acoustics is the study of the physics of sound, which concerns vibrating strings or air columns, fundamentals, overtones, and the like. In this booklet the term *acoustics* will be used the way most musicians use it: in reference to room acoustics and the reaction to sound within a space where it can be reflected, absorbed, or reverberated according to basic physical laws. The room in which sounds are generated has a large effect on those sounds. Therefore the acoustics of a room become an essential element in the use of that room for music instruction, practice, or performance.

* * *

Sound Reflection and Absorption

Sound waves that strike room boundaries are absorbed or reflected depending on the shape and composition of the surfaces. The listener and performer receive a mix of direct and reflected sound. Proper balance between these two, especially in a performance room, is very important. Sounds are influenced by the room area, volume, and geometry, and by the reflective or absorptive nature of the walls, floor, and ceiling. Furnishings and occupants in the room also affect the room's acoustics.

The first step toward providing a supportive environment in a large performance space is to surround the performers with nearby sound-reflective surfaces. Although an acoustical shell enhances the music, a true concert hall sound also requires reverberation: the lingering of sound after the source ceases. The effect of reverberation—or lack of reverberation—on the quality of instrumental and choral sound is well recognized.

Music by different composers, of different music periods, for different instruments or kinds of ensembles is heard at its best in particular acoustical environments. For instance, the music of Giovanni Gabrieli is enhanced by a space with a long reverberation time.

The larger the space or the less sound-absorbing material in that space, the longer the sound can reverberate. A large space is ideal for performance of choral or organ music. Smaller or less reverberant spaces are more appropriate for drama and the unreinforced spoken word.

* * *

Appropriate Acoustics

Musicians sometimes say that they desire a rehearsal room that sounds like a performance hall. But rehearsal rooms should not try to duplicate the sound of an auditorium because they are teaching classrooms where clarity and definition are more important than flattering listening conditions.

Though important, reverberation time is not the only element of good acoustics. Attention should also be given to qualities such as freedom from intruding sounds, quiet electrical and mechanical systems, adequate area and volume, and quiet lighting. Also very important is the proper mix of direct and reflected sound, which depends on the shape of the room and the materials that make up the interior surfaces.

Often music must be performed in spaces planned for speech and vice versa. If we place speech in an overly reverberant space, the lingering of the sound causes syllables to overlap and blur. On the other hand, music performed in a dead, dry theater will also be dry and lifeless. If a rehearsal or performance room must serve more than a single purpose it must incorporate acoustical adjustability if it is to work optimally for all uses.

The acoustics of a space should complement the activities carried on within it. Many existing facilities simply were not designed for the various facets of music teaching and performing. These facilities become liabilities rather than assets to the music program. Fortunately, many flaws in music rooms can be minimized or corrected. Don't placidly accept flaws. Try to correct them for your own benefit and the benefit of your students.

All music rooms, not just performance areas, should have good acoustics. This booklet addresses common acoustic problems in music classrooms, practice rooms, rehearsal rooms, and performance areas and examines how to make the most of new or existing spaces.

* * *

Critiquing Your Music Rooms

To help you decide if your rooms are a help or a hindrance to your music program, you should assess them against some standard. MENC provides a section on facilities for three grade levels—elementary, middle/junior high, and high school—in *The School Music Program: Description and Standards* (MENC, 1986). This information is also found in the appendix of *Music Facilities: Building, Equipping, and Renovating* (MENC, 1987).

The following questions can immediately help you in your evaluation. Go through them and check your response in the column to the right. If you often answer no, you should be alerted to the negative status of your facilities.

Rate Your Rehearsal Room

		Yes	No
1.	Is your room large enough to accommodate your largest class or ensemble comfortably?	☐	☐
2.	Is the volume of the room large enough to accommodate the greatest sound power level of your largest group and to provide enough liveness and reverberation to enhance the musical effect? (The cubic footage, area times height, should be close to 500 cubic feet per student for band or orchestra and 250–300 cubic feet for choral groups.)	☐	☐
3.	Is lighting quiet and free from buzzing or humming?	☐	☐
4.	Is the heating and ventilating system quiet and unobtrusive?	☐	☐
5.	Is the floor flat and seating flexible, especially in band and orchestra rehearsal rooms, or, if there are risers, are they portable units?	☐	☐
6.	Is the ceiling high enough to provide space for the music to be enhanced and mixed and to accommodate the greatest sound power level of large, mature groups? (The ceiling should be 15–16 feet high for choir and 20–22 feet high for band and orchestra, and higher for	☐	☐

very large high school or college
ensembles.)

7. Is the rehearsal room live enough so that the   ☐   ☐
music does not sound dead and lifeless?

8. Is the rehearsal room dead enough so that   ☐   ☐
reverberated sound is not deafening and
details are clear at full volume, making effec-
tive teaching easier?

9. Can you hear all instruments and voices and   ☐   ☐
all details?

10. Can students hear themselves and hear   ☐   ☐
"across the ensemble" so they can be sensitive
to intonation, balance, and blend?

Rate Your Practice Rooms

11. Are practice rooms and private teaching stu-   ☐   ☐
dios isolated properly from adjacent rooms?

12. Is lighting and ventilation quiet?   ☐   ☐

13. Are the acoustics within the rooms accept-   ☐   ☐
able?

Rate Your Performance Room

14. Is the performance room a real auditorium   ☐   ☐
and not a gymnasium or cafeteria?

15. Does it have adequate and variable acoustics   ☐   ☐
with adjustable draperies or other elements?

16. Is lighting quiet?   ☐   ☐

17. Is heating and ventilation quiet, with twice the   ☐   ☐
number of air exchanges compared to a regu-
lar classroom?

18. Is the performance area (stage) surrounded by   ☐   ☐
sound-reflective surfaces (such as a shell) and
not heavy, sound-absorbing stage curtains?

Rate Your Music Classroom

		Yes	No
19.	Does the classroom encourage good singing practices and music making through its live acoustics?	☐	☐
20.	Is 70–80 percent of the ceiling hard and sound reflecting to provide this favorable environment?	☐	☐
21.	Are the ventilation and lighting systems quiet?	☐	☐
22.	Is your classroom one designed especially for teaching music? (If no, see the following.)	☐	☐

If you are teaching in a room not designed for music, review all of the qualities referred to in questions 19–22 and make a list of any treatments needed to make the room ideal for music. Or make a list of all the compromises that remain in not accommodating the many specialized requirements for music study.

The most frequent shortcomings of rooms not designed for music are inadequate size, low ceilings, improper acoustics (too dead), noisy ventilation, and poor sound isolation. *Note that many of these inadequacies can be improved.*

* * *

Upgrading Acoustic Weaknesses

The previous list of questions and answers can be useful in planning a new space as well as in evaluating and upgrading an existing one. Follow through on your "no" answers and be aware that many of them can be changed to a "yes." While it is seldom possible to raise the roof or move walls, it has been done.

* * *

A Few Hints

Control sound in an overly live room by adding absorptive panels or acoustical draperies. A dead room can be brightened by sealing absorptive surfaces and removing carpet and draperies.

* * *

Add acoustical flexibility to a multipurpose room by adding acoustical draperies that can be retracted for choir and extended for band or orchestra.

* * *

Add clarity and the ability to hear details in a too-reverberant room by adding acoustical panels on the walls.

* * *

Noisy florescent lamp ballasts can be replaced with electronic or Type "A" sound-rated ballasts that are quiet, or the ballasts can be moved to a remote closet where their buzzing will not be annoying.

* * *

Control intruding sounds from adjacent rooms by beefing up the walls, caulking all leaks or openings in walls or ceilings, and by adding sound seals to the doors.

* * *

Quiet noisy ventilation to some degree by installing lined ducts and silencers in the duct runs and, in some cases, by changing the pulleys on fans and motors. Reduce vibration noise by adding isolators on all vibrating mechanical equipment.

* * *

General Tips

Compensating for poor acoustics is difficult if not impossible, which is one reason a good acoustical environment is so important in the first place. In a space at either extreme—one that is dead and dry or live and overly reverberant—hearing across the ensemble is poor at best so the players must depend more than usual on visual clues from the conductor. In a dry space, sounds seem to fall at your feet, so extra effort and forced tone production often result. In a "wet" space, lowering dynamic levels can reduce ringing and echoes to make the sound more acceptable. Some other helpful hints follow.

* * *

Facilities

Cafetoriums are seldom good spaces for music performance. In designing a new one, plan it as a music space in which food can be served rather than an eating place in which music must be performed. Performing in a gymnasium works best acoustically if the performing group sets up across the width of the gym, not the length. Also, rolling out carpet, both under the performers (especially in a band or orchestra) and between the ensemble and the audience, will cut down on the big "boom." In the typical gymnasium, it will help to muffle the bass drum and have the bass instruments play lightly.

* * *

Auditoriums for multipurpose use should be planned using an "open stage" design that places performers and audience in one room without an intervening proscenium arch. Acoustical and cost advantages to this approach can be considerable and accommodations for music, drama, and other uses can readily be made.

* * *

Other Performance Settings

Performing outdoors can require sound reinforcement and amplification. If possible, line the ensemble up against an outside wall of a building to provide nearby sound reflections; the ensemble will hear themselves better and the sound will project to the audience better, too.

Lacking such a convenient wall where you are to perform, try to obtain a portable stage and acoustic shell on a trailer unit, or try to set up at least some sections of an indoor stage shell to wrap around the rear and sides of the ensemble to improve listening conditions for performers and listeners alike.

Risers are very helpful if there is no convenient hill or bank on which the outdoor audience can be seated. This allows sound to project over the heads of the audience in front to those in the rear who are usually seated on a flat surface. Good sight lines are good sound lines. Sound grazing over the heads of patrons in front rows rapidly decreases in volume.

* * *

Performances in shopping malls expose music groups to large if transient audiences. Often the performance occurs in a center court with a high ceiling and big space around the performers. Here, too, as in a gymnasium concert, use a shell wrapped around the sides and rear of the performers to conserve and direct sound energy and also to improve communication across the ensemble.

* * *

Acoustic Tools

Stage sound shells serve many useful purposes, including separating performers from absorptive stage curtains, improving stage communication (hearing across the ensemble), and more efficiently projecting sound to the audience.

* * *

Draperies for acoustical control and adjustability must be thick and heavy (20–25 ounces per square yard) or they will not control sound adequately. Stage curtains should retract into pockets or be removed to get them out of the sound field for musical performances.

* * *

Amplification of musical instruments is commonly restricted to those designed and built with their own amplifiers, such as electronic guitars, keyboards, and synthesizers. Amplifying a concert ensemble is tricky, although not impossible. Amplification does help in certain situations indoors, but it must be done with taste and skill.

10

To be completely natural, sound reinforcement systems should have point-source identification—the sound should seem to come directly from the source and not from the side or above it. These systems should be carefully designed using a consultant who can outline specifications and test for compliance with them. Vendors should be experienced in commercial sound system design and installation, and not only in home stereo or amateur radio systems. The output of the system should be compatible with the natural acoustics of the space and with the demands of its intended uses.

* * *

Multimedia functions in today's schools may require engaging a relatively new specialist, a media consultant. This individual could integrate audio, video, cable television, and computer functions in all music rooms and, using fiber optic cable, interconnect them with a campus-wide system.

* * *

How to Proceed

Don't expect someone else to take the initiative for upgrading your existing rooms or for expert planning of new ones. *You* have to be the initiator and promoter, bringing the needs to the attention of your school administration and carefully bringing whatever pressure you can to bear. Interested music parents who sit on the school board can help a great deal. No other department is in a better position to display its work to the public and engender the public's support.

* * *

Help from a Professional

One method that works well in many cases involves the music director, who, sensing inadequacies, enlists the support of the music booster club to bring in a consultant at the club's expense. If possible the consultant should have wide experience in school or college music work. He or she can analyze the school's accommodations and compare them to the prescribed standards established by MENC's *The School Music Program: Description and Standards.* A report should be written for school board review and approval. This report should also go to a contractor for cost estimating. The music booster organization pays for the study, or works to encourage the school board to pay for such a study. The school board then pays for the actual improvements on an existing building or for an adviser or consultant to work from the earliest planning stages of a new facility to its completion.

To emphasize: *You* must be the one to approach the administration and be personally involved in the entire project if it is to be successful. *Every good facility has a school staff member who was dedicated to the pursuit of excellence in its design.*

* * *

Conclusion

This *TIPS* booklet has been developed to give you a summary of what a good music facility offers and to provide a method for evaluating yours. It is hoped that this information will strengthen any proposal that may be brought forth to improve the facilities. If you are fortunate enough to be involved in planning new music spaces, this book should give you insight into the highly specialized requirements needed to make music rooms work well.

Sources of more detailed and, in some cases, more technical information are listed under Resources (page 16). The books mentioned should be in your school or personal library and should be consulted as more complete resources.

While much can be accomplished by using these materials as guides, it is best to have an experienced music facility planner and acoustical consultant employed as early as possible on any project. In the long run, money will be saved and the project will be properly directed from the start.

One tends to rely on architects' expertise, but because music facilities are constructed infrequently, few architects have much experience with them. Every project is different. What works in one case may not necessarily work in another.

* * *

Glossary of Acoustic Terms

By Edward McCue

Sound **absorption** can be compared with light absorption. Just as sunlight is absorbed by a black velvet jacket, a portion of the sound of an orchestral horn section is absorbed when it is positioned in front of stage curtains.

Sound **diffusion** is similar to the effect of light being scattered when it bounces off a piece of white paper. The sound of a trumpet played into ranks of organ pipes is diffused in many directions.

Echoes are produced when distant surfaces reflect sound to a listener long after the direct sound from the original source has been heard. Trombonists on stage can often produce echoes off the back wall of an auditorium.

Flutter arises when a sound source is situated between parallel, sound-reflecting surfaces. A rim shot played on a snare drum in an untreated rectangular classroom will produce the prolonged, buzzing sound of flutter.

Frequency is the physical description of musical pitch. A thick carpet absorbs a portion of the high-frequency sounds of a piccolo but has little effect on the low-frequency energy of a tuba.

Excessive **loudness** occurs when an ensemble plays in a room that is too small or acoustically untreated.

Masking occurs when a noise conflicts with a musical sound similar or higher in pitch. Building mechanical system noise can mask the sound of basses and cellos in an orchestra rehearsal hall.

Sound **reflection** off a hard, flat surface can be compared to the reflection of light off a mirror. Choirs often stand back from the edge of a stage so that their sound can be reflected off the platform into the audience.

Reverberation is the buildup of reflected sound in an enclosure that affects the character and quality of music. The sound of a band in a fieldhouse is reverberant because it is reflected many times before it dies away. The same music played outdoors does not reverberate because there are no walls or ceiling to contain it.

Resources

Egan, David M. *Architectural Acoustics*. New York: McGraw Hill, 1988. This book is only for the more technically minded music teacher who wants a deeper understanding of acoustics from the scientific aspect. Covers basic theory, room acoustics, sound absorption, sound isolation, mechanical system noise and vibrations, speech privacy, and electronic systems. Contains the sort of information the acoustical consultant deals with regularly, presented here in a useful and accessible format.

Geerdes, Harold P. *Music Facilities: Planning, Equipping and Renovating*. Reston, VA: Music Educators National Conference, 1987. The current MENC guide to music buildings and equipment, this book has proved helpful to hundreds of schools, colleges, and universities planning building renovation or construction. It is the only comprehensive manual on the subject. The appendix includes the facilities standards information from MENC's *The School Music Program: Description and Standards*.

McCue, Edward, and Richard H. Talaske. *The Acoustical Design of Music Education Facilities*. New York: Acoustical Society of America, 1990. This excellent volume is a treasure house of information in both narrative and photographic form. Contains a series of eleven essays on various aspects of acoustical design along with photographs and technical information describing fifty music building projects since 1975. An exhaustive bibliography lists books and articles on the subject and a detailed index cross references every detail of information contained in the text. An invaluable resource for anyone who is serious about building new facilities and doing it right.

The School Music Program: Description and Standards 2d ed. Reston, VA: Music Educators National Conference, 1986. This publication contains, in addition to its standards in curriculum offerings, a section on standards for music facilities at elementary, middle school and junior high school, and high school levels. For each level both a basic program and a quality program are outlined.

The National Council of Acoustical Consultants (66 Morris Avenue, PO Box 359, Springfield, NJ 07081, telephone 201-379-1100) is the professional organization of qualified consultants who adhere to the highest standards of professional excellence. The organization offers advice on which services to expect from an acoustical consultant and how to go about choosing one from its complete directory.

About the Authors

Harold P. Geerdes is associate professor of music emeritus at Calvin College in Grand Rapids, Michigan, where he maintains a consulting service. MENC members are welcome to contact him for general advice and help on any school or college music facility project. He is a member of MENC, the American Federation of Musicians, and other music organizations, as well as the Acoustical Society of America, the National Council of Acoustical Consultants, and the Audio Engineering Society.

Edward McCue is an acoustical consultant on the staff of R. Lawrence Kirkegaard Associates in Boulder, Colorado.